SARMATARVM AMAXOBIIS ARMATE

xviii. P Tricorno .vii. Monte aureo xiiii. Margum — o R viminatio .x. xiii. Punicum .xi. vico cuppe .vii. Arcidaua

PRIOR Ledonara .xv. apo. ft.

va. xviiii. Stanecli Argentaria MESIA

Sanderua .vi. Vars .xv. Salunto xviiii. Halata .x. Dersunno .xvi. Sinna .vi. Municipio .v. Iouis pago .xii. idimo

Resinum .xx. Vicinum .xv. Batua Sco BRC Adpicaria .xxx. Creueni .xvii. Gabuleo .xxx. Theranda

Pistum .xxv. Bycratio .xv. A

Melit lis Lues CRIS Deruee lis Sisonis Genesis fl .xx. Hapsum fl .xxvi. Clodiana

Pastium Baletium .xv. Lippa .xxv. Ydrunte .vii. Castru Minerue .xii. Apollonia .xxx. Autona .xvi.

Brundis Manduris .xxx. Beretum .x. Baletium .x. Vnitum .v. Veretum ALE

Vrbius .x. Tarento .xv. Neretum

Melochoro .x. Brunento Tortiboli Heraclea .iii. Semnum Turis .xxviii. Petelia Cibutona .vi. Lacenium Annibali

Grumentum .xvii. Grater H colonia .xx. Temsa Ω

Capraia .xv. Crater fl Aquae Angae H Tanno Sellatio Caulon .xxx. Lues

BRITTIVS Annea .vii. Scolec

Blanda .xvi. Lauinium .viii. Cerelis .xl. Lumpeia .x. Temsa .viii. Tanno Vibona Baletria .xviii. Taurata .vii. Arcabe .vii.

Tannod lis lis Lipara Regio v. Leucopetra

Vulcani lis Strongile Leucopetra

Cephaledo xviii. Halesa .vii. Calacte .xii. Agatunno .xxx. Tindareo .xxvi. Messana

Enna .vii. Aguro .vii. Centuri fa .vii. Tauromenio fl. Siciminu

Acilua A Petri Bagreouos H

labodes vi. Agrigento .xl.viii. Calunsiana .xxviii. Bible .xviii. Agris .xv. Siracusis

osa col.

ΘΕVΦ MARE Sabitta Pontos .xiii. Assaria .xx.

Ventuo Adcypsaria Taberna .xxvi. Adamonem .xvi. xxvii.

Haribus Frehicto .xv. Pisida Municipio .xx. C fl Ausere BAGIETVLI

Rufini Taberna

xxv. Ausere fl Porea Taurini veri fl Girin

Endpapers: a copy, made in the 1200s, of a map which shows the world as known to the Romans. stretching from India to Britain. The land is lighter green separated by the darker strips of the Mediterranean and Adriatic Seas.

Library of Congress Cataloging-in-Publication Data

Briquebec, John.
    The ancient world.

    (Historical atlases)
    Summary: Describes historical and social events in various parts of the world from the era of the first known prehistoric people through the fall of the Roman Empire.
    1. History, Ancient—Juvenile literature.
    [1. History, Ancient]   I. Title.   II. Series.
    D57.B87   1990   930   89-24915
    ISBN 0-531-19073-0

Published in 1990 by Warwick Press,
387 Park Avenue South, New York, New York 10016.
First published in 1989 by Kingfisher Books Ltd.
Copyright © Grisewood & Dempsey Ltd. 1989.

Library of Congress Catalog Card No. 89-24915
ISBN 0-531-19073-0

Editor: Nicola Barber
Series editor: Ann Kramer
Series designer: Robert Wheeler
Cover design: Nigel Osborne
Maps: Eugene Fleury and Malcolm Porter
Illustrations: Kevin Maddison
Additional illustrations: Vanessa Card, Stephen Conlin
Picture research: Elaine Willis
Phototypeset by Rowland Phototypesetting Ltd, Bury St Edmunds, Suffolk
Printed in Spain

HISTORICAL ATLAS

THE ANCIENT WORLD

From the Earliest Civilizations to the Roman Empire

John Briquebec

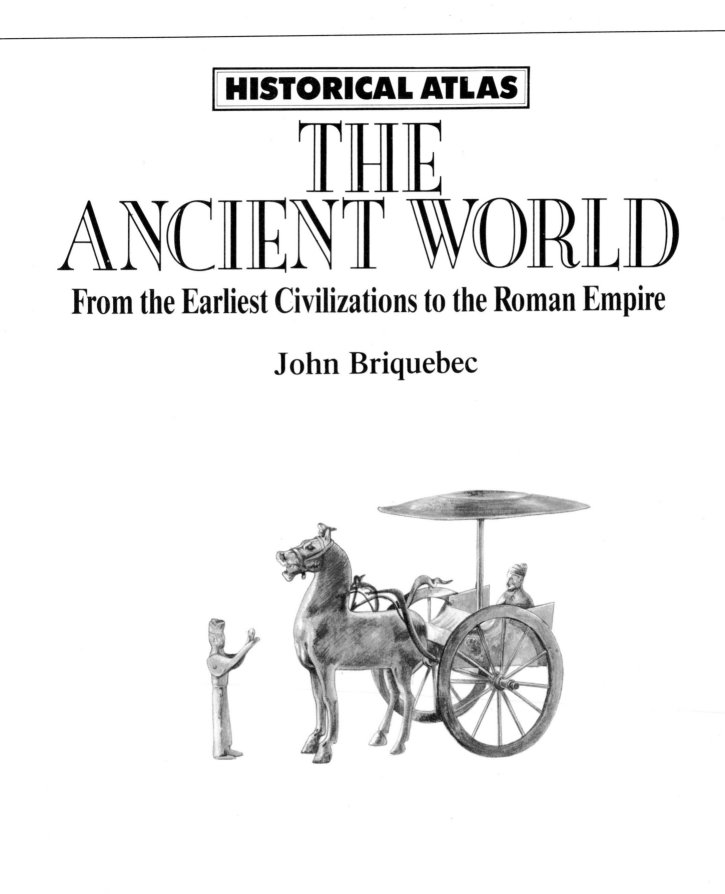

WARWICK PRESS

Contents

Peoples of the West and South

Introduction

This book tells the story of the history of the Ancient world. It begins when the earliest peoples lived on Earth and ends with the rise of the great empires of Greece, Rome, and China. It examines how farming began, how writing developed and looks at the first civilizations to emerge.

But history is not just about empires and civilizations. It is also about how people lived in the past—what they believed in, what they ate, and how they dressed. Using clear maps and colorful pictures, *The Ancient World* describes the daily lives of Ancient peoples such as the Egyptians, Phoenicians, and Chinese, as well as explaining the impact of major events upon their lives.

The Ancient World is divided into five chapters. The first chapter looks at the work of archaeologists, and explains how we can understand the lives of the very earliest peoples even though they left no written records. The following chapters each describe the history of one particular region of the world. Feature pages cover important aspects, such as the development of writing and birth of some of the world's major religions. Difficult words and terms, which are in **bold** in the text, can be found in the Glossary, while the Timeline at the end of the book gives an overview of the whole period.

The Earth is Peopled

History is what people write down about the past, and the way in which it is interpreted. But to find out about life before written language was invented, about 5,000 years ago, we have to rely on **archaeology**, the study of what people leave behind them—their buildings, the tools they used, the clothes they wore, their pottery, and paintings. Scientists can measure very accurately when objects were made and used, so we can learn a surprising amount about the **culture** of these long-dead people—that is, the way they lived, what they believed and how they behaved.

Scientists called **anthropologists** use the remains of people themselves to show how humans developed from a group of mammals called the **Primates**, which also includes the great apes, gorillas, and chimpanzees. The earliest traces of **hominids**—people-like creatures—have been found in Africa and are given the scientific name *Australopithecus* meaning "southern ape." The oldest-known fossil of *Australopithecus* was found in Ethiopia in 1981 and is four million years old. Modern people, whose scientific name is *Homo sapiens*, have existed for at least 300,000 years.

▲ Finding out about the past on a site in Peru. Archaeologists set out a grid so that they can locate and record accurately any "finds" that they come across. In this way they can learn more about the people who made the things they discover.

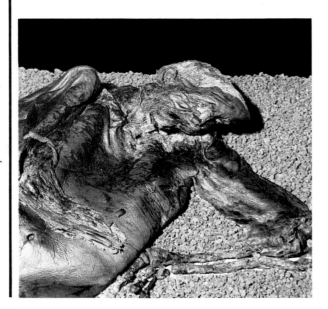

◄ When archaeologists dig up the remains of ancient humans they usually find only **fossilized** skeletons. But the body of this man was discovered at Lindow Moss in Cheshire, England, with the skin still intact, preserved by the bog in which it was found. He was murdered about 2,000 years ago, perhaps as a religious sacrifice.

30,000–8000 B.C.

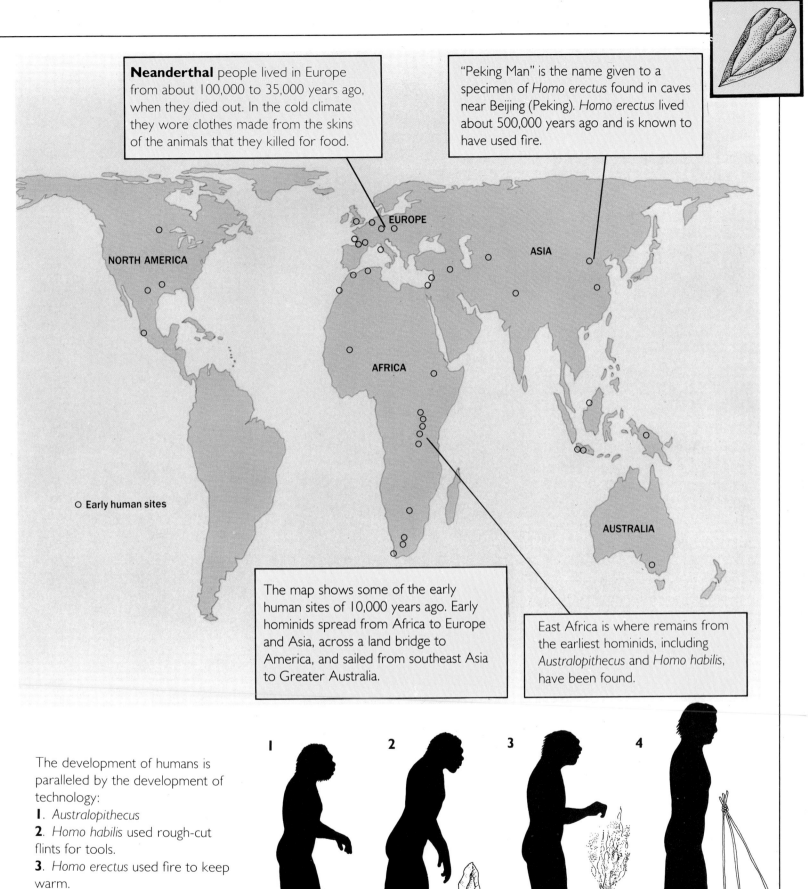

Neanderthal people lived in Europe from about 100,000 to 35,000 years ago, when they died out. In the cold climate they wore clothes made from the skins of the animals that they killed for food.

"Peking Man" is the name given to a specimen of *Homo erectus* found in caves near Beijing (Peking). *Homo erectus* lived about 500,000 years ago and is known to have used fire.

EUROPE

ASIA

NORTH AMERICA

AFRICA

○ Early human sites

AUSTRALIA

The map shows some of the early human sites of 10,000 years ago. Early hominids spread from Africa to Europe and Asia, across a land bridge to America, and sailed from southeast Asia to Greater Australia.

East Africa is where remains from the earliest hominids, including *Australopithecus* and *Homo habilis*, have been found.

The development of humans is paralleled by the development of technology:
1. *Australopithecus*
2. *Homo habilis* used rough-cut flints for tools.
3. *Homo erectus* used fire to keep warm.
4. *Homo sapiens neanderthalis* used a bolas for hunting. When thrown at a running animal the bolas wrapped itself around the animal's legs and brought it down.

1　　　2　　　3　　　4

30,000–8000B.C.

The ice ages

The way in which people spread around the world was affected by climate. The past million years have seen a series of **glacials** (ice ages) with warmer spells, called **interglacials**, in between. At the height of the glacials, ice sheets covered northern Europe, Asia, and north America and made it too cold for human settlement. But during the warmer interglacials people began slowly to adapt to the colder temperatures farther north, by finding shelter and making fire, tools, and clothes. The first people to survive the colder climate of western Europe were the Neanderthals—so called because their remains were first found in the Neander Valley (*Tal*) in West Germany. They lived between 100,000 and 35,000 years ago on areas of land bordering the great glaciers.

The ice that covered the land during the glacials took water from the seas and oceans, and as a result the sea level fell by several yards. This meant that land which had been covered by water was exposed, and people could migrate across **land bridges** to new areas. So the first people to reach America probably trekked from Siberia to Alaska about 40,000 years ago. In southeast Asia people went, probably by raft, across what were then very shallow seas to New Guinea, and from there traveled on foot over a land bridge to Australia where they settled at least 50,000 years ago.

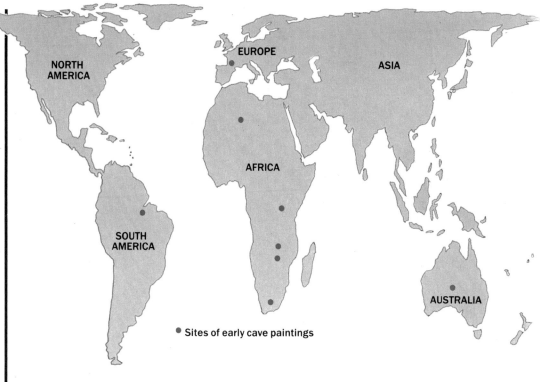

• Sites of early cave paintings

▲ The map shows where early cave and rock paintings have been found. *Homo sapiens* painted them between 35,000 and 10,000 years ago. The animal drawings may have been part of a magical ritual connected with hunting.

▼ Part of a wall-painting discovered in a cave in Lascaux, France. The animals on this wall were painted between 19,000 and 18,000 years ago. The oxen have been drawn in black outline; the horses and deer have been filled in with a color.

30,000–8000B.C.

▼ This carving of a female figure holding a bison's horn was found in a cave at Laussel, France. It is between 30,000 and 15,000 years old. Several figures like this have been found in France and southern USSR. They are often called "Venuses" because they are thought to represent mother-goddesses.

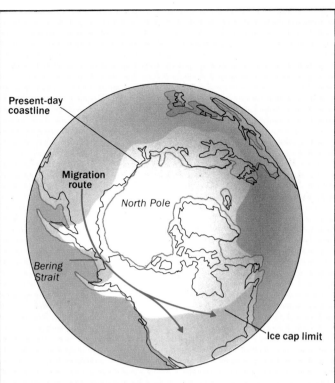

The map shows the southernmost limit reached by the ice cap in the last ice age (the Würm period). During the ice age a huge amount of water was frozen into the ice cap: in places the ice cap was 10,000 feet thick. As a result the level of the world's oceans fell by more than 300 feet and there were land bridges in many places where there is now sea. Animals migrated across these land bridges, followed by the humans who hunted them. In this way early humans reached America.

◀ At first tools were made by rubbing two stones together to produce an edge on one. But using a piece of bone or stone to press flakes off a flint meant that a greater variety of tools could be produced.

1. A knife-like blade
2. A borer
3. A point

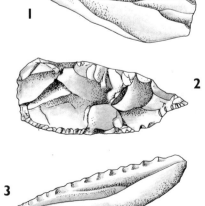

30,000–8000 B.C.

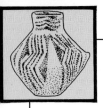

The Fertile Crescent and its Neighbors

The hunter-gatherers

The people who roamed the Earth 500,000 years ago hunted animals and gathered whatever nuts, fruits, and other vegetable matter they could find for food. When the supply of food in one place ran out, or when the herds of animals moved on, the people had to move too. Collecting or catching enough food to stay alive took up everybody's time.

The first farmers

What changed people's lives, over many generations, was the gradual development of **agriculture**. Slowly, people discovered that certain plants could be grown or cultivated to provide crops, and certain animals could be protected or domesticated to provide meat, milk, hides, or wool. Gradually, many people began to rely on the steady supply of food from their crops and animals, and instead of moving from place to place to gather their food, they started to settle in fertile areas of land.

Some of the earliest farmers settled, nearly 10,000 years ago, in what is often called the "Fertile Crescent." This was an area of land which was well watered by the Tigris, Euphrates, and Nile Rivers. Here people grew wild wheat and wild barley, and kept goats, sheep, pigs, and cattle.

▲ Without water crops cannot grow, so a system of watering cultivated land, or **irrigation**, is very important. Different methods were used by different peoples. In this picture the ox is turning a wheel to raise pots of water from a larger channel to a smaller one.

▶ The goat was one of the first animals to be domesticated and kept for its milk.

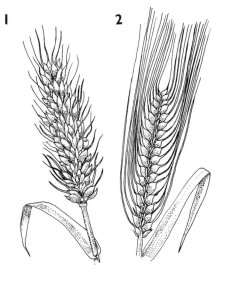

◀ The first grains to be cultivated were various types of wheat (**1**) and barley (**2**). The early farmers harvested wild grains and then sowed the seeds they obtained, watering them and fertilizing them to give fatter seed grains.

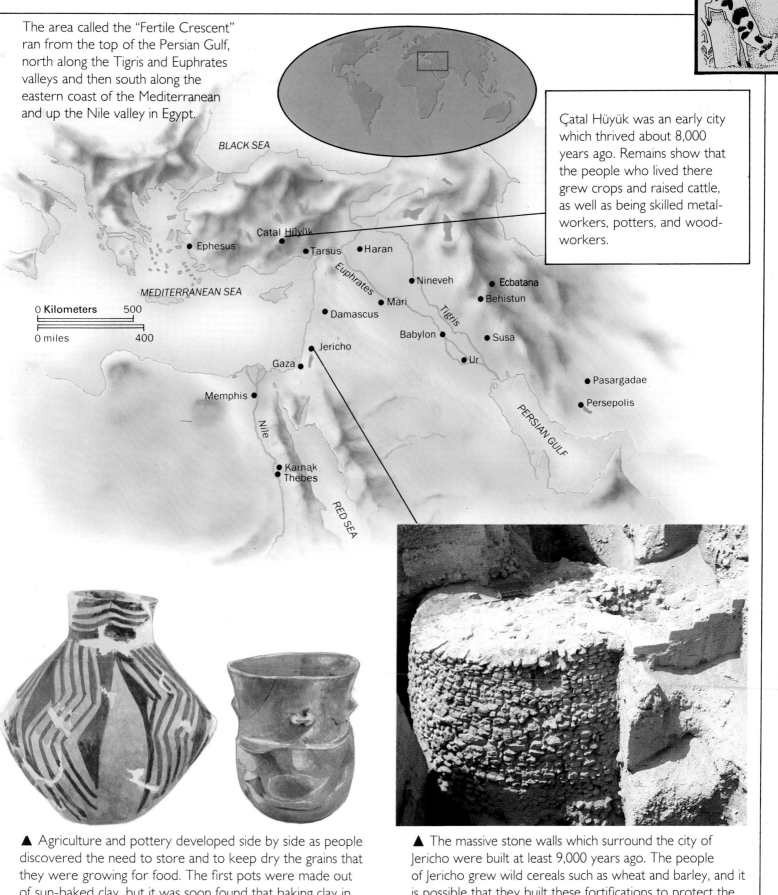

The area called the "Fertile Crescent" ran from the top of the Persian Gulf, north along the Tigris and Euphrates valleys and then south along the eastern coast of the Mediterranean and up the Nile valley in Egypt.

BLACK SEA

MEDITERRANEAN SEA

0 Kilometers 500
0 miles 400

Ephesus
Çatal Hüyük
Tarsus
Haran
Euphrates
Nineveh
Ecbatana
Mari
Behistun
Damascus
Tigris
Babylon
Susa
Jericho
Ur
Gaza
Memphis
Pasargadae
Persepolis
Nile
PERSIAN GULF
Karnak
Thebes
RED SEA

Çatal Hüyük was an early city which thrived about 8,000 years ago. Remains show that the people who lived there grew crops and raised cattle, as well as being skilled metal-workers, potters, and wood-workers.

▲ Agriculture and pottery developed side by side as people discovered the need to store and to keep dry the grains that they were growing for food. The first pots were made out of sun-baked clay, but it was soon found that baking clay in the fire made it harder and longer-lasting. These pots were found at an early settlement near Çatal Hüyük, and they were made about 7,800 years ago.

▲ The massive stone walls which surround the city of Jericho were built at least 9,000 years ago. The people of Jericho grew wild cereals such as wheat and barley, and it is possible that they built these fortifications to protect the store of grain which they had gradually accumulated. The city was attacked, burned, and then rebuilt many times until its final destruction about 3,500 years ago.

The first civilizations

After many generations settlements grew and became established, in some areas people began to coordinate and organize their beliefs, **trade**, and government: and as a result, the first **civilizations** emerged.

The earliest civilizations of the Fertile Crescent were in Mesopotamia, the land between the Tigris and the Euphrates Rivers. The first people to settle in Mesopotamia were the Sumerians. After about 3500B.C. they established centers of civilization in towns and cities, called "**city states.**" In each of these city states was found a royal palace, a temple tower (**ziggurat**), and an administrative center, around which were houses, and beyond them the fields and marshlands of the farmers. One of these city states, Ur, became very powerful because of its trade: cloth and ready-made clothes were produced in the city's workshops and exchanged for copper, gold, ivory, and timber.

Around 2000B.C. the power of Ur was weakened, and a **nomadic** people from the north, the Amorites, took over the land where the Tigris and the Euphrates converge and established a center called Babylon. However, Babylonia was conquered by the Assyrians, a warlike nation from the city state of Assur, with a trained and organized army, skilled horsemen, and weapons made from **bronze** and iron.

14

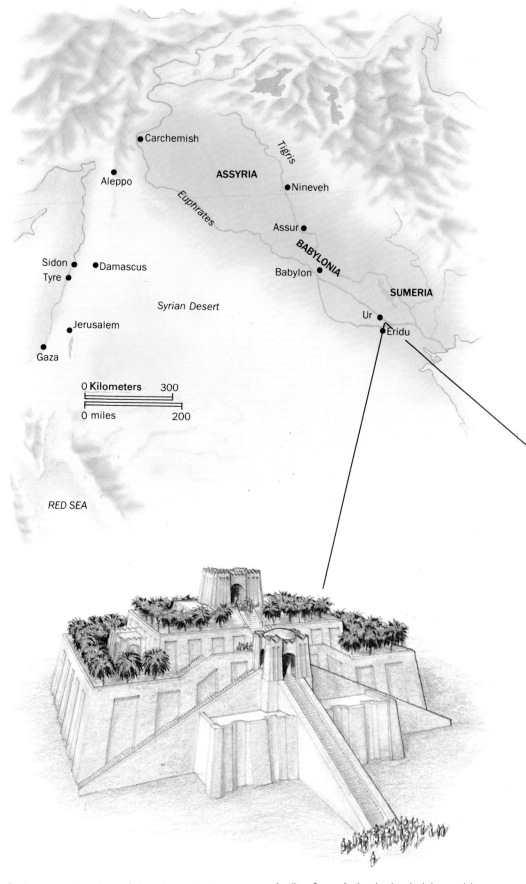

▲ A reconstruction of the ziggurat at Ur. On the top was a temple where the king performed religious rites and sacrifices with the high priestess of Ur. It was built of sun-baked, clay bricks and it may have been decorated with glazed tiles (not shown here). It was finished in about 2100B.C.

▲ Part of the impression from a limestone cylinder **seal** made in Mesopotamia between 5,500 and 5,000 years ago. Seals were used to identify property. The upper part of the impression shows some cattle; below is a byre (shelter for animals).

▲ The Marsh Arabs of southern Iraq still build and live in reed houses, just as the farmers in the marshlands of Mesopotamia did. The houses are similar in construction to the byre shown on the seal (*above, left*).

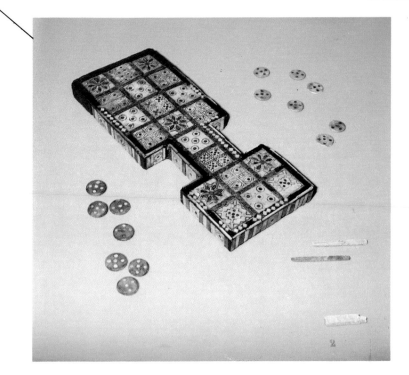

▲ A board game, complete with dice and counters, made and used in Ur about 4,500 years ago. The Mesopotamians were skilled mathematicians; from them we inherit the method of dividing up time into 60 seconds, minutes, and hours, and a circle into 360 degrees.

Mesopotamia
*c.*8000B.C.: first development of agriculture.
*c.*3500B.C.: the Sumerians begin to develop their civilization.
*c.*3200B.C.: earliest writing.
2800B.C.: the first Semitic people settle in Mesopotamia.
2360B.C.: Akkadian Empire founded by Sargon.
1792–1750B.C.: rule of Hammurabi, king of Babylon.
*c.*1750B.C.: rise of Babylonian Empire.
*c.*721–705B.C. Assyrian Empire at height of its power.
689B.C.: Babylon destroyed by Assyrians.
539B.C. Nabonidus, last king of Babylonia, surrenders to Cyrus the Second of Persia.

The Ancient Egyptians

Like the people of Mesopotamia, the Ancient Egyptians established their settlements on fertile land along a river, the river Nile, more than 5,000 years ago. There were two **kingdoms** — Lower Egypt in the delta area at the mouth of the Nile, and Upper Egypt in the south, but these were united in 3200B.C. by the **Pharaoh** (king) Menes, who was the first in a line of Pharaohs who ruled Egypt for the next 2,500 years. Whereas the various kingdoms of Mesopotamia, based around city states, remained relatively small, the kingdom of Egypt flourished under one rule, with a single system governing the whole land.

At the top of this system was the Pharaoh. He was considered to be a god, and commanded the service and goods of all his subjects. The belief that, as gods, the Pharaohs continued to live after death led to the building of the pyramids. In these huge tombs the Pharaohs were buried with everything they might need in the afterlife, including food. The immense power that the Pharaohs wielded over their people is shown by the time, the number of workers, and the wealth needed to build these tombs.

Egyptian farmers

At the other end of the social system were the peasant farmers who worked in the fields. Egyptian agriculture relied on the annual flooding of the Nile River which, when the

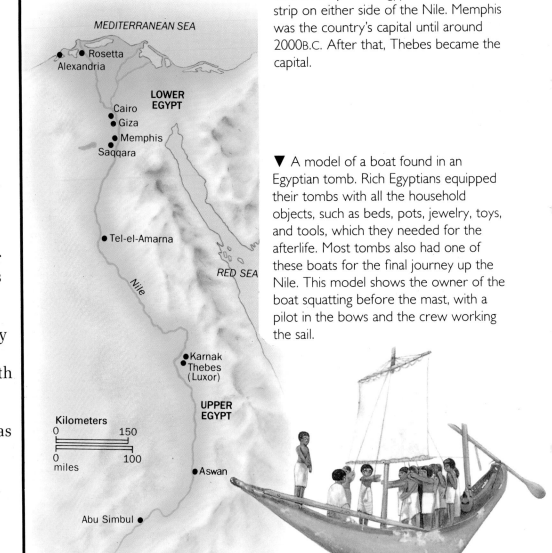

The fertile part of Egypt was a narrow strip on either side of the Nile. Memphis was the country's capital until around 2000B.C. After that, Thebes became the capital.

▼ A model of a boat found in an Egyptian tomb. Rich Egyptians equipped their tombs with all the household objects, such as beds, pots, jewelry, toys, and tools, which they needed for the afterlife. Most tombs also had one of these boats for the final journey up the Nile. This model shows the owner of the boat squatting before the mast, with a pilot in the bows and the crew working the sail.

▼ A section through the Great Pyramid at Giza, near Cairo, the largest of the Pyramids. It was constructed with 2,300,000 blocks of stone, each weighing an average of 2½ tons. Some of the stone was quarried nearby, but some of it was brought by river from Aswan and dragged on rollers from the river's edge. The Ancient Greek historian, Herodotus, records that 100,000 people toiled for 20 years to build it as a tomb for Pharaoh Khufu, who died in 2567B.C.

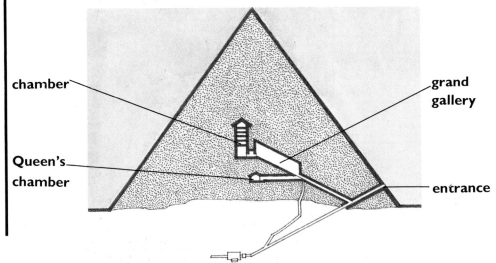

▲ A wall-painting from the tomb of Menna at Thebes.

▲ Scenes from a modern reconstruction of an Egyptian village. The ordinary people who worked in the fields were often paid barely more than they needed to live on, and a large percentage of the harvest was taken away in tax.
Top Winnowing: trampled ears of grain are picked up in flat wooden scoops and tossed high into the air to separate the chaff (which blows away) from the wheat (which falls to the ground).

▶ Egyptian men wore a simple linen kilt, knotted around the waist. It was sometimes ornamented with pleating at the front. Official and ceremonial dress was more complicated—for example, priests wore leopard skins.

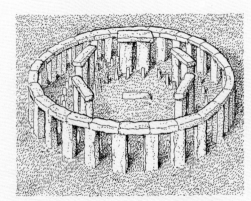

Did you know that Stonehenge in England was begun at about the same time as the Great Pyramid in Egypt?

17

water level had subsided, left behind it fertile silt in which crops such as wheat, barley, and flax could be grown. Wheat and barley were used to make bread and beer, and flax provided the linen with which the Egyptians made most of their clothes. Meat was a luxury for most Ancient Egyptians, but cattle were reared for their dairy produce, as beasts of burden,and for ritual slaughter.

Egyptian people

In between these two extremes were many levels of Egyptian society such as the **viziers** and supervisors close to the Pharaoh at court, priests in the temples, merchants, and craftspeople. Scribes were particularly important because they oversaw the harvest and recorded the yield of the crops; they also wrote down the history of their times and inscriptions glorifying Egyptian victories in war.

The population of Ancient Egypt was spread among the towns and small villages along the Nile. The most important settlements were the royal cities chosen by the Pharaohs, such as Memphis and Thebes. Next in importance were the *nome* (provincial) centers, which were local centers for administration and taxation.

All the buildings except, of course, the Pyramids and some of the temples which were built of stone, were made of unbaked mud-brick — a mixture of Nile mud and straw, shaped in a wooden mold and left to dry in the sun.

▲ The Egyptians worshiped many gods and goddesses and they also believed in magic to guard against evils. This magic wand, made from hippopotamus ivory, was used to protect the owner against poisonous creatures, such as snakes and scorpions, at night.

◀ When the Pharaoh died his body was preserved by a process called mummification in order for it to continue on its journey in the afterlife. The body was swathed in bandages and enclosed in a highly-decorated mummy-case like the one shown here. Later, rich Egyptians also received this treatment.

▼ This tomb model of a man shows him filtering a fermented mixture to make beer. Beer was the main drink in Egypt. It was made from barley and stored in beer jars.

The Spread of Writing

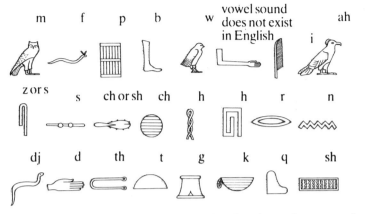

As civilizations emerged and trade developed, people began to record information by writing it down. The first writing we know of comes from Mesopotamia as early as 3200B.C. Here the Sumerians drew little pictures on clay tablets, probably in order to keep records and accounts of their goods for trading. Gradually over the next 200 years these "pictograms" were replaced by patterns made by a chopped-off reed on soft clay: each pattern stood for a sound or syllable. This type of writing is called cuneiform (meaning wedge-shaped). It lasted from about 3000B.C. to A.D.75, several centuries longer than our own writing has been in use!

Although they knew of cuneiform, the Egyptians developed their own more elaborate picture-writing called "hieroglyphs." Like the Sumerians, the Egyptians gradually developed a system in which their pictograms stood for sounds rather than things. However, the Egyptians also invented a new and more convenient material on which to write—sheets of papyrus made from the papyrus reed, from which comes our word "paper."

The first surviving specimens of Chinese writing were found on the oracle bones of the Shang dynasty (see page 23). Over 2,000 different characters have been found on these bones and it is obvious that writing was already well developed in China by this time. The Chinese language developed in a completely different way from the western languages, using the shapes of characters to represent things and ideas, not syllables or sounds.

▲ Egyptian hieroglyphs: some of the signs have the value of one letter of our alphabet, others represent two letters or more.

◄ Writing on a soft clay tablet with a reed pen

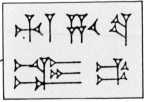

Cuneiform

Chinese characters

Indus valley glyphs

Egyptian hieroglyphs

The Persians

The last of the early civilizations of this region was in Persia (Iran). Two nomadic tribes, the Medes and the Persians, moved southward from the area which is now southern USSR about 2,900 years ago. In 549B.C. a Persian king, Cyrus the Great, conquered the Medes and set about creating a huge **empire**. The Persians were good riders and they used iron weapons. Within only 30 years they had expanded their empire to cover the whole of Mesopotamia, Anatolia (Turkey), the eastern Mediterranean, and what are now Pakistan and Afghanistan.

However, it was left to a later Persian king, Darius the Great, to devise a system of government which would hold together this huge empire. The Empire was divided into 23 (later 31) administrative regions, called **satrapies**, each with a governor (*satrap*) who controlled a region, but who also had to make gifts of cereals and other produce to the Persian king. Roads were built, including the Royal Road, to link together the various parts of the Empire. They were also used for trade — traders transported and sold raw materials, clothes, carpets, and spices. In 520B.C. Darius introduced a standardized currency to be used throughout the Empire, which also encouraged trade.

The Persian Empire flourished until 331B.C. when it was conquered by Alexander the Great of Macedonia.

▲ This tiny gold model of a Persian chariot is part of the "Oxus treasure" found in Afghanistan. It shows the kind of vehicle in which Persian nobles traveled on business along the roads of the Empire. The Persians were skilled craftspeople, renowned for their fine work in gold and silver.

Both these impressions were taken from seals which were rolled across moist clay to produce signatures to identify property.

▲ This seal was probably the property of one of Darius's highest officials, and shows the king in his chariot, hunting lions.

◄ The ordinary people of the Empire rarely appeared on seals. This one shows a man plowing with his team of oxen.

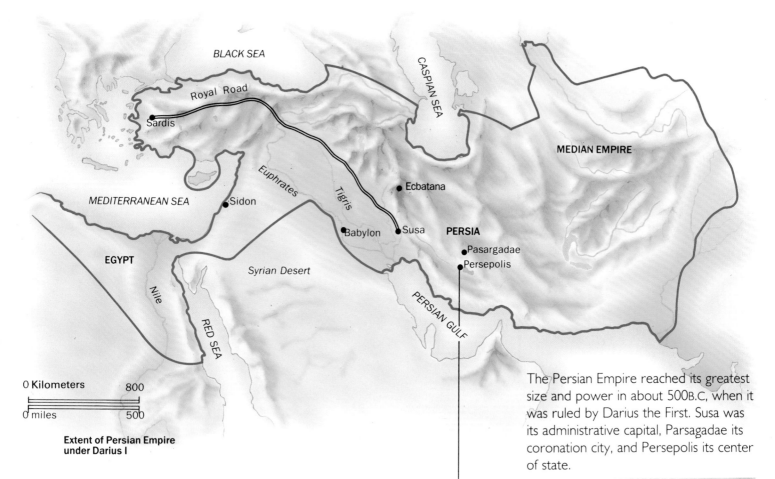

BLACK SEA

Royal Road

Sardis

CASPIAN SEA

MEDIAN EMPIRE

Euphrates

MEDITERRANEAN SEA

Sidon

Tigris

Ecbatana

Babylon

Susa

PERSIA

Pasargadae

Persepolis

EGYPT

Nile

Syrian Desert

RED SEA

PERSIAN GULF

0 Kilometers 800

0 miles 500

Extent of Persian Empire under Darius I

The Persian Empire reached its greatest size and power in about 500B.C, when it was ruled by Darius the First. Susa was its administrative capital, Parsagadae its coronation city, and Persepolis its center of state.

▶ An aerial view of the ruins of Persepolis as they stand today in southern Iran. Darius the First ordered the start of building work in 520B.C. Persepolis was only used by the "King of Kings" and his court once a year during New Year, when tribute was brought to him by the peoples of his Empire.

▶ Assyrians bearing tribute to the "King of Kings" at the New Year ceremony. They bring dressed animal skins and a pair of rams chosen from their flocks.

Civilizations of Eastern and Southern Asia

Ancient China

The earliest civilizations of Ancient China grew up on the banks of its three largest rivers: the Huang He (Yellow River), the Chang Jiang (Yangtse), and the Xi Jiang (West River). Like the peoples of the Fertile Crescent, the Chinese farmers relied on the rivers for water to grow their crops, and for transport, but devastating floods were always a threat. There was also the danger of invasion from the north by the Xiung-Nu (Huns or Mongols). As a result, the building of waterworks, and of defenses against human attacks were important features of China's early history.

The Shang

The first **dynasty**, or ruling family, of which we are certain was called the Shang. Their capital city seems to have been moved — maybe as a result of both floods and invasions. However excavations at one of the cities, An-yang, revealed wooden houses in which most people lived, as well as palaces, store rooms, and tombs of the kings and people of rank.

People of the Shang Dynasty grew millet, wheat, and some rice and kept domesticated animals such as cattle, pigs, sheep, dogs, and chickens. Silk was already an important cloth, but it was worn only by

▲ A reconstruction of an early Chinese house of about 2000 B.C. It probably housed one family. The roof was supported by wooden uprights, and traces of such uprights have been found by archaeologists excavating sites near the Huang He (Yellow River) in northern China.

▶ A pottery model of a watchtower made around A.D 100. This model was made for the tomb of a wealthy person in the Han period.

Ancient China

c.1500 B.C.: Shang Dynasty (Bronze Age culture).

1027 B.C.: Chou Dynasty.

c.650 B.C.: introduction of iron working.

551 B.C.: Confucius born.

221 B.C.: Ch'in Dynasty (first united empire).

202 B.C.–A.D.220: Han Dynasty (rise of Confucianism).

c.112 B.C.: opening of "Silk Road" linking China to the West.

50 B.C.–A.D.50: Buddhism introduced from India.

AD 220–587: Six Dynasties period.

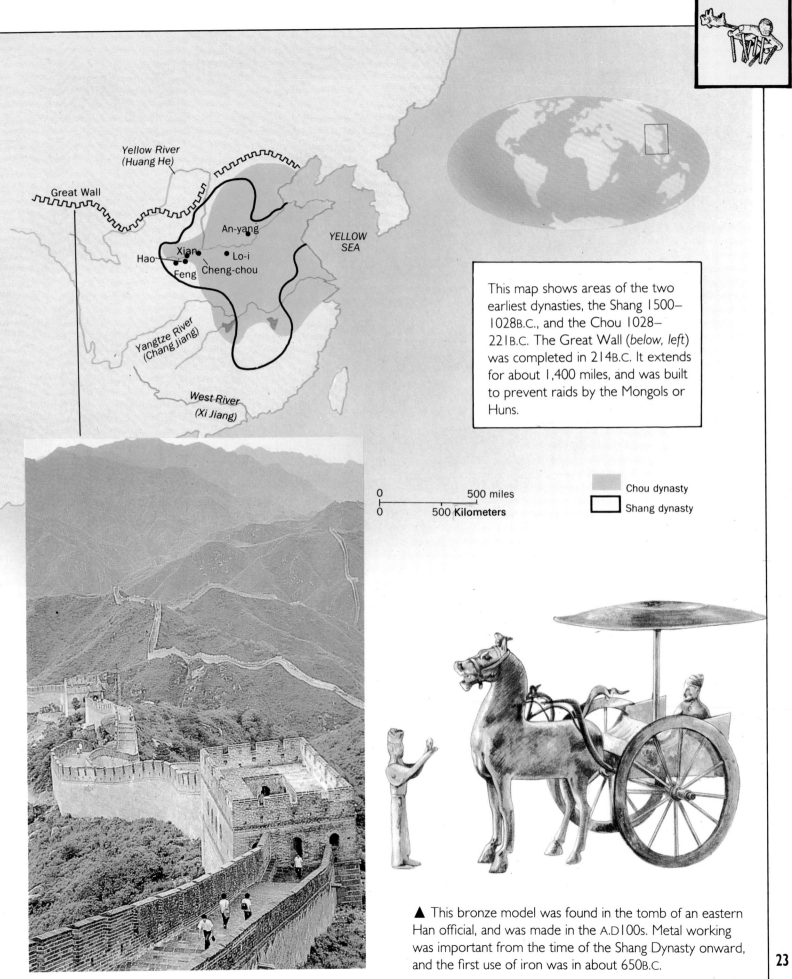

Yellow River
(Huang He)

Great Wall

An-yang

Xian
Hao
Feng
Cheng-chou
Lo-i

YELLOW
SEA

Yangtze River
(Chang Jiang)

West River
(Xi Jiang)

This map shows areas of the two earliest dynasties, the Shang 1500–1028B.C., and the Chou 1028–221B.C. The Great Wall (*below, left*) was completed in 214B.C. It extends for about 1,400 miles, and was built to prevent raids by the Mongols or Huns.

0   500 miles
0   500 Kilometers

Chou dynasty
Shang dynasty

▲ This bronze model was found in the tomb of an eastern Han official, and was made in the A.D100s. Metal working was important from the time of the Shang Dynasty onward, and the first use of iron was in about 650B.C.

23

the rich—ordinary people wore linen or cotton.

The dynasty came to an end when nomadic groups from the west took over, establishing the Chou Dynasty. They introduced the working of iron (in about 650B.C.), and whereas the Shang had used metal—usually bronze—only for ornamental purposes, now iron was used for weapons and for agricultural tools such as plows. This made cultivation much easier.

The Ch'in Dynasty

In 221B.C. a Ch'in king, Shih Huang Ti, pronounced himself Emperor and founded the Ch'in Dynasty. He unified his vast empire by standardizing weights and measures, introducing a uniform coinage, and by improving the network of roads and canals.

Nineteen years later, the Ch'in Dynasty was succeeded by the Han Dynasty which ruled—with a short interruption—until A.D.220.

Japan

The development of civilizations was slower in Japan, mainly because of this island country's isolation. Fishing provided much of the food needed and the early Japanese, the Jomon, also cultivated grains, such as rice, and kept domestic animals. After about 100B.C. the Yayoi culture arose. Its people used bronze and iron to make decorative objects, but still used stone knives and simple wooden containers.

▲ The excavated tomb of Shih Huang Ti near the village of Xian in Shaanxi province. Thousands of life-size pottery figures and horses have been found guarding the tomb of the Emperor. The faces of the figures and horses are all different and may be portraits of actual people and animals.

▼ A reconstruction of the Izumo shrine in Japan, a temple of the Shinto religion. Seasonal ceremonies were held here to ensure good crops, fertility, and health.

Did you know that since ancient times the Chinese have used bones as oracles, to try to foretell the future? Questions to the gods were carved onto the bones. When the bones were heated cracks appeared across the written characters and gave the gods' answers.

Religions and Beliefs in Eastern Asia

Three of the world's main religions and beliefs began in eastern Asia: Hinduism, Buddhism, and Confucianism.

Hinduism

Hinduism is the world's oldest surviving religion and is still the main religion of India. It is not known exactly when and where it began, but the origins of Hinduism lie in the religion of the Aryan people who settled northern India from 1500B.C. onward (see *page 26*).

Archaeologists know little about these people but what they do know has been learned from their literature which was passed down by word of mouth for many centuries. The most important early work of this literature was the *Rig-Veda* which became a holy book for all Hindus. The *Rig-Veda* is a collection of hymns which were originally chanted by the Brahmans or priests at sacrifices. It was not written down until A.D.1300.

The three most important Hindu gods are Brahma, creator of the Universe, Vishnu, who preserves the Universe, and Shiva who destroys it.

Buddhism

Buddhism also originated in northern India. It was founded by a prince called Siddhartha Gautama who was born in 563B.C. to a life of wealth and luxury. When he was 29 he left his family and rejected his comfortable life. Dressed as a beggar he wandered from place to place. Starting from the traditional teaching of the Hindu Brahmans he rejected their ritual and sacrifice and instead began to teach a method of disciplining both mind and body in order to attain *Nirvana*, a state of perfect peace and happiness. He was called Buddha, "the Enlightened One."

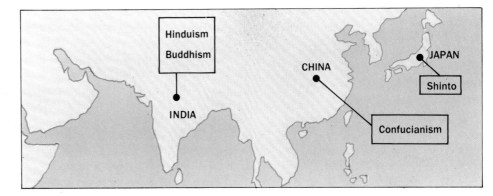

Confucianism

Confucianism is a way of life and moral behavior rather than a religion. It is based on the teachings of a Chinese wise man who lived from 551 to 479B.C. He was called Kung Fu-tzu which was translated into Latin as Confucius. As a young man he worked as an administrator for a prince, but he withdrew from

▼ There are many statues and carvings of the Buddha but none are from his own time.

▲ The teachings of Confucius influenced the development of Chinese civilization for two thousand years.

active life and began to meditate on questions of right and wrong. His "system" was that people's lives should be ruled by a principle of order: doing good meant finding your place in that order and respecting the places of other people and things in it.

The teachings of Confucius were adopted by the rulers of the Chinese empire as the official philosophy; they also spread to Korea and Japan.

The traditional religion of Japan is Shinto which is more than 2,500 years old.

The Indus valley civilizations

The early peoples of India inhabited sites around the Indus and Ganges Rivers, but the first civilization to emerge was in the Indus valley in about 2500 B.C.

The two largest cities of the Indus valley civilization were Mohenjo-daro and Harappa. At the center of both was an artificial mound or **citadel**, with a large well-ventilated granary in which grain was stored. At Mohenjo-daro there was also a bath-house, with cells and private baths surrounding a large bath which may have been used by priests. Beyond the citadel the workers' houses were built in well-planned rows, with streets crossing at right angles and a system of drains and sewers. The houses were built around a courtyard with several rooms, a well, and a toilet. All of the buildings were made with bricks, baked in wood-fired ovens.

The huge granaries at Harappa and Mohenjo-daro suggest that the livelihood of the Indus valley people was based on farming—wheat and barley being the main crops. They also traded goods, such as cotton, probably with the peoples farther west in Mesopotamia.

The Indus civilization seems to have ended quite suddenly in about 1500 B.C., possibly when its cities were attacked by **Aryan** invaders from the north. No single civilization took its place until the Mauryan Empire emerged in central India in about 320 B.C.

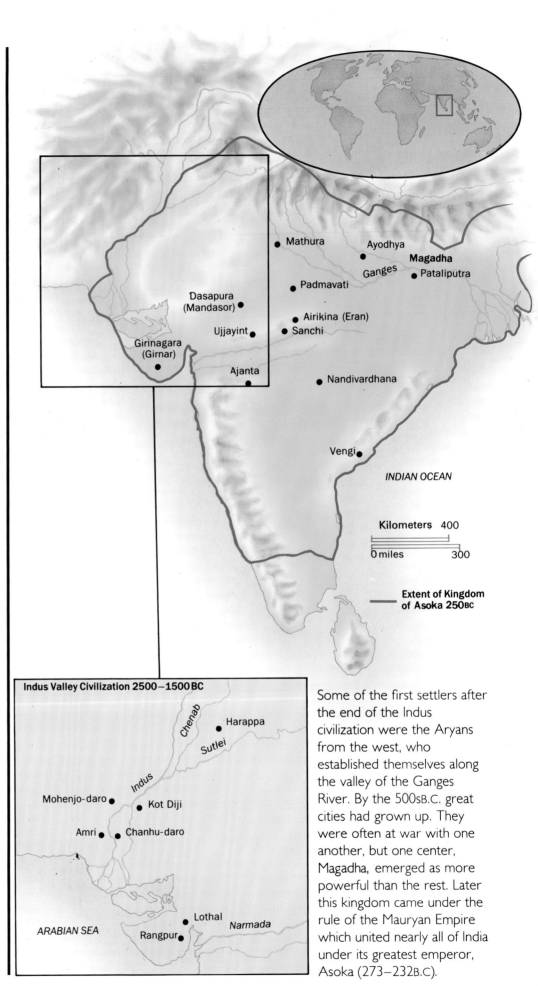

Indus Valley Civilization 2500–1500 BC

Kilometers 400

0 miles 300

Extent of Kingdom of Asoka 250 BC

INDIAN OCEAN

ARABIAN SEA

Some of the first settlers after the end of the Indus civilization were the Aryans from the west, who established themselves along the valley of the Ganges River. By the 500s B.C. great cities had grown up. They were often at war with one another, but one center, Magadha, emerged as more powerful than the rest. Later this kingdom came under the rule of the Mauryan Empire which united nearly all of India under its greatest emperor, Asoka (273–232 B.C.).

▶ The impressive ruins of the city of Mohenjo-daro. The buildings were carefully planned out on a grid design, and built with **kiln**-baked bricks. These bricks were of such good quality that many of them were taken away and used in the A.D 1800s to build railway embankments.

▼ Brick-lined shafts like this are found in the courtyards of many of the houses in Mohenjo-daro. They may have been wells or storage places for vases or jars.

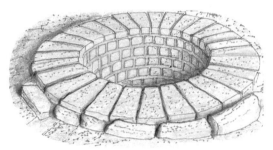

▼ Over 1,200 of these seals have been found in the ruins of Mohenjo–daro. They were used by merchants to stamp bales and other property. Many of them have animal designs and show the great variety of wild animals known to the Indus valley people: elephants, tigers, rhinoceroses, antelopes, crocodiles, and humped bulls.

◀ This **terracotta** statuette of a mother-goddess figure was found at Mohenjo-daro. She is wearing a loincloth and jewellery.

Ancient India

c.2500 B.C.: Indus valley civilization begins to emerge.
c.1500 B.C.: collapse of Indus valley civilization.
c.1500 B.C.: Aryans settle in northern India and ? destroy Indus valley civilization.
c.800 B.C.: Aryan settlement expands southward.
563 B.C.: birth of the Buddha.
327 B.C.: Alexander the Great dies.
c.320 B.C.: Mauryan Empire founded in northern India.

Civilizations of Europe and the Mediterranean

The civilizations that succeeded those of Mesopotamia and Egypt grew up around the shores of the Mediterranean Sea.

The Israelites

The Israelites were a **Semitic** people related to both the Babylonians and the Assyrians. They migrated to Palestine in about 2000 B.C., and after a period of exile in Egypt, returned to Palestine. Here, under King David, they set up a kingdom, with its capital at Jerusalem. Later, Palestine was split into two hostile kingdoms, Israel and Judah.

The Phoenicians

From 1200 B.C. the Phoenicians established themselves along the eastern shore of the Mediterranean, where they cultivated wheat, barley, olives, vines, and figs. Their main centers were the ports along the coast, such as Tyre and Sidon, from where they sailed all over the Mediterranean, trading goods — timber, glassware, metalwork, and ivory. In time they **colonized** much of the Mediterranean shore, the largest and most famous colony being Carthage.

One of the Phoenicians' most important exports was the purple cloth which gives them their name (Phoenicia comes from the Greek *phoinos*

▲ Masada is a natural rock fortress near the Dead Sea. It was developed by Herod the Great, king of Judea, as a fort with storehouses, baths, a synagogue (meeting place), two palaces, and enough space in the center to grow some crops. In A.D. 72–73 a group of patriotic Jews (Zealots) made a final stand at Masada against the Romans.

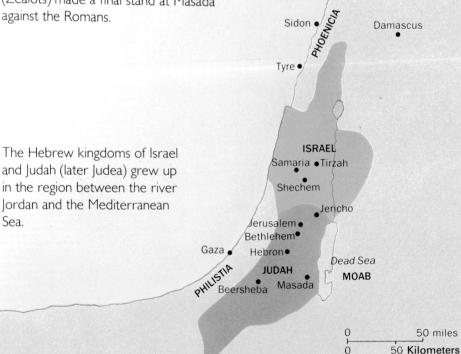

The Hebrew kingdoms of Israel and Judah (later Judea) grew up in the region between the river Jordan and the Mediterranean Sea.

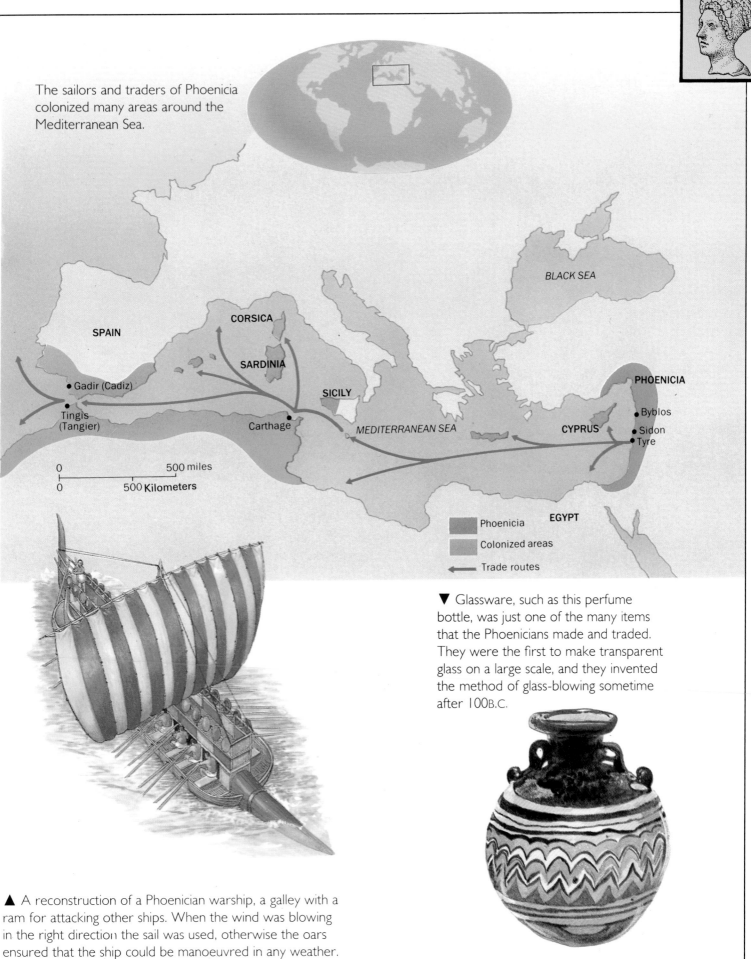

The sailors and traders of Phoenicia colonized many areas around the Mediterranean Sea.

BLACK SEA

SPAIN

CORSICA

SARDINIA

SICILY

PHOENICIA

Gadir (Cadiz)

Tingis (Tangier)

Carthage

MEDITERRANEAN SEA

CYPRUS

Byblos

Sidon

Tyre

0   500 miles

0   500 Kilometers

Phoenicia

Colonized areas

Trade routes

EGYPT

▼ Glassware, such as this perfume bottle, was just one of the many items that the Phoenicians made and traded. They were the first to make transparent glass on a large scale, and they invented the method of glass-blowing sometime after 100 B.C.

▲ A reconstruction of a Phoenician warship, a galley with a ram for attacking other ships. When the wind was blowing in the right direction the sail was used, otherwise the oars ensured that the ship could be manoeuvred in any weather.

meaning purple). The dye for the cloth was made from a substance produced from shellfish. The vivid purple color of the cloth became a symbol of authority in the Roman Empire.

Minos and Mycenae

The first European civilization was established on the island of Crete after about 2000B.C. The Minoan civilization was named after its legendary king, Minos. The Minoans built several large cities which were connected by a network of roads. Each of these cities centered around a palace, the largest and grandest being at Knossos, where there were royal apartments for the king and queen, rooms for religious rites, workshops for the skilled Minoan craftspeople, and a "schoolroom" where pupils learned to read and write in order to become scribes.

The brilliant Minoan civilization came to an end suddenly in about 1450B.C. Whether it was destroyed by an earthquake or taken over by the Mycenean Greeks is not certain.

The Mycenean Greeks established a civilization in southeast Greece at the same time as the Minoans, and were at first influenced by them. However, the Myceneans were more warlike; their cities were built like fortresses and they accumulated wealth not only by trade but also by plundering and raiding. They traded around the Mediterranean, importing copper and tin to make bronze, as well as

▼ A death mask of beaten gold from a tomb at Mycenae. When it was first found it was described as the mask of the legendary king Agamemnon. The Myceneans buried their kings and nobles in shaft graves, sunk vertically into solid rock. Beside the bodies they laid objects of bronze, gold, ivory, pottery, and silver. Later tombs were made by tunneling into hillsides.

▼ A room in the palace at Knossos showing some of the frescoes which cover the walls of the palace.

continued on p.32

▼ The ruins of the Parthenon in Athens. The Parthenon was built between 447 and 438B.C and it was designed to impress by its size and splendor. Inside, the temple housed a finely-worked statue in gold and ivory of the patron goddess of the city, Athene. There was an altar outside at which people worshiped, and where sacrifices were possibly made.

▲ This little bronze statue of a girl athlete trom Sparta is part of a lid of a vase found in Yugoslavia. Whereas Athenian girls were kept at home and taught how to be good housewives, girls from the city-state of Sparta were encouraged to lead much freer lives.

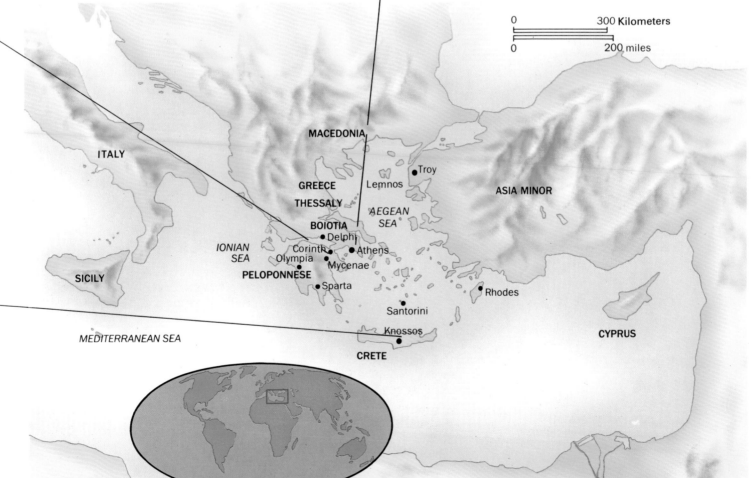

ITALY

MACEDONIA

GREECE

THESSALY

BOIOTIA

Delphi

IONIAN SEA

Corinth

Olympia

Athens

Mycenae

PELOPONNESE

Sparta

SICILY

Troy

Lemnos

AEGEAN SEA

ASIA MINOR

Rhodes

Santorini

Knossos

CRETE

CYPRUS

MEDITERRANEAN SEA

0   300 **Kilometers**

0   200 miles

precious stones and metals. In exchange, they exported bronze weapons, jewelry, olive oil, wine, and wool.

Athenians and Spartans

The importance of the Myceneans decreased after about 1100B.C. In the mountainous Greek countryside city states gradually grew up on the small plains between the mountains. Communication was often difficult between the city states, so each small state developed separately and had its own government and laws, and often its own army, currency, weights and measures. Each city state was governed by an **aristocratic** family. Around the central city or *polis* of each state were the villages and farms of the ordinary people where they grew wheat, olives, and vegetables, and reared goats for cheese and milk.

Two of these city states grew in importance: Sparta and Athens. The Athenians developed the idea of **democracy**, by which they meant that the people took a direct part in government. But "the people" included only the Athenian male **citizens**: women, slaves and people who were not Athenians had no political rights.

In 481B.C. Sparta and Athens united to fight a war against a common enemy—Persian invaders. But later in the same century (431–404B.C.) they fought each other in a war which was eventually to ruin Athens.

▲ The picture on this *amphora* or vase shows a racing chariot with four horses at the Games. The Olympic Games were originally held as a religious ceremony in honor of Zeus. Women held their own games in honor of the goddess Hera. The Olympic Games were held every four years from 776B.C. to A.D.261. In 520B.C. the timetable for the events was as follows:

Day 1: sacrifices, oaths, checking of athletes.
Day 2: equestrian events, pentathlon.
Day 3: religious observations, boys' events.
Day 4: "track" events, wrestling, boxing, race in armor.
Day 5: banquet, sacrifices.

◀ While marble statues often portrayed heroic figures of gods and goddesses, little clay figures portrayed the everyday life of ordinary people. This figure was made in 500B.C. and shows a woman grinding grain to make bread. Bread was the staple diet in most Greek towns, but eggs, vegetables, olives, grapes, and figs were also grown and eaten. Meat was usually only eaten after a sacrifice.

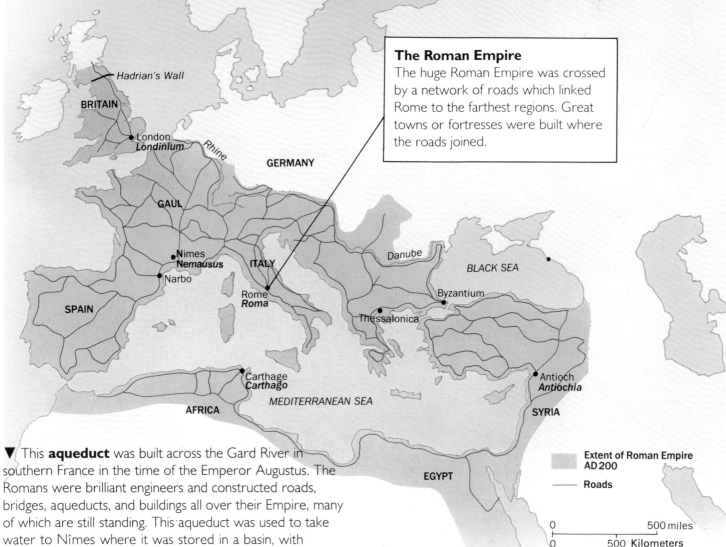

The Roman Empire
The huge Roman Empire was crossed by a network of roads which linked Rome to the farthest regions. Great towns or fortresses were built where the roads joined.

Extent of Roman Empire AD 200

Roads

0   500 miles
0   500 Kilometers

▼ This **aqueduct** was built across the Gard River in southern France in the time of the Emperor Augustus. The Romans were brilliant engineers and constructed roads, bridges, aqueducts, and buildings all over their Empire, many of which are still standing. This aqueduct was used to take water to Nîmes where it was stored in a basin, with controlled outlets to both civic and private users.

▶ The ruins of the Colosseum, a huge **amphitheater** in the center of Rome. It was officially opened in A.D.80 and could hold 50,000 spectators. Both men and women came to watch the bloodthirsty fights to the death between gladiators (usually prisoners-of-war or condemned criminals), or between wild beasts. Beneath the floor of the amphitheater were underground cages for the wild beasts, and a water system to flood the area for mock sea battles.

The Romans

The first civilization in Italy was that of the Etruscans who established small, independent city states in the area which is now called Tuscany. We know little about the Etruscans, but they undoubtedly influenced their southern neighbors, the Romans, passing on, for example, their skill in building roads.

Rome itself was originally an Etruscan city but in 509B.C. the local aristocrats or "patricians" expelled the Etruscan king and set up a **republic**. At first the patricians governed Rome: they elected two **consuls** from among themselves who were advised by the **Senate**. But gradually the ordinary people or "plebeians" became more powerful and demanded a part in the government of Rome. After 367B.C. it became the custom for one consul to be a plebeian.

By 44B.C. the Romans ruled the whole Mediterranean world, either directly or by influence over native rulers. They linked together their huge Empire with a network of roads, and controlled it with a well-disciplined army. Trade flourished as the Roman way of life became established in many parts of the Empire: wine, olive oil, wool, linen, and silk, spices, fine pottery, and glass were all traded within the Empire.

The Roman Republic ended in a **civil war** in which one man, Octavian, gained supreme power. He was given the title Augustus and created himself Emperor.

▲ Part of Trajan's Column which tells the story of two of the wars fought by the Roman army under Trajan's command. The soldiers were well-trained and not only fought battles but also built bridges and fortresses; here they are building a camp, some soldiers are digging a double ditch, while others construct ramparts out of squared pieces of turf.

▶ A Roman family at dinner. The men recline on a couch to eat. Slaves stand by to wait on them.

▼ In his shop the Roman butcher wields a cleaver similar to those used today. His wife sits in a chair doing the accounts.

Religions of the Mediterranean Lands

Three important modern religions began close to the Mediterranean Sea: Judaism, Christianity, and Islam. Unlike the eastern religions (see page 25) all three are based on a belief in one God.

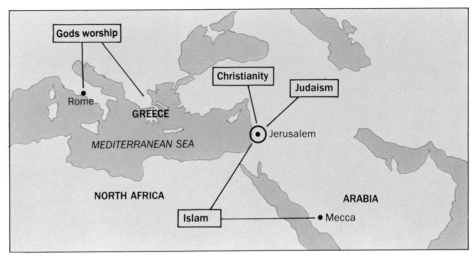

Judaism

Judaism is the religion of Israel, and has been the religion of the Jews all over the world for more than 3,000 years. Jews believe in one God whom they call *Yahweh* and he is the creator of all things.

The basis of Judaism is the Ten Commandments which, according to tradition, God gave to the Jewish leader Moses some time in the 1200sB.C. The commandments and laws based on them rule every aspect of Jewish life. The history and laws of the Jews are contained in the Old Testament of the Bible.

▲ A mosaic of the seven-branched candlestick or Menorah. A golden Menorah stood in the tabernacle, the Jew's first holy temple.

Christianity

For centuries the Jews have believed that a Messiah (savior) would be born to lead them. At the time that Jesus of Nazareth was born, around 4B.C., the Jews were under Roman rule. Jesus's followers believed him to be the promised Messiah, the son of God, but other Jews accused him of blasphemy, and he was tried before the Roman governor of Judea, Pontius Pilate. Jesus was crucified, probably in about A.D30, but his followers (disciples) reported having seen and talked to Jesus after his death. This resurrection formed the basis of the new religion that arose from the old traditions of Judaism: Christianity.

The life and teachings of Jesus are contained in the four Gospels of the New Testament of the Bible.

Islam

Islam is a much younger religion than either Judaism or Christianity. It was founded in the A.D.600s by the Prophet Muhammad. Muhammad was born in Mecca, an important trading center in Arabia. At that time most Arabs believed in nature gods, spirits

▼ The Dome of the Rock, a Muslim mosque in Jerusalem. Jerusalem is a holy center for Jews, Christians, and Muslims.

and demons. One day, Muhammad was sitting outside a cave when he heard a voice telling him to set down the words of God. His writings over the next 22 years were put together to form the Koran—the holy book of Islam.

The followers of Islam are called Muslims which means "those who submit." Muslims worship one god, Allah, and they have strict religious observances including regular prayer.

Peoples of the West and South

Although the civilizations of Europe and eastern Asia lay far apart, they were linked by traders, even in ancient times. But there were two regions of the world which were completely cut off from the rest: the Americas and the Pacific. A third, Africa south of the Sahara, had comparatively few links.

The Americas
The first people to reach America probably walked across a land bridge where the Bering Strait now is (*see page 11*). The early Americans were hunters, fishers, and food gatherers. They used stone tools and although metals such as gold, silver, and copper were worked with hammers the secret of **smelting** was never discovered. Iron was not introduced into America until the European invasion in the A.D.1500s.

Farming began in an area called "**Mesoamerica**" by archaeologists, which includes central America and Mexico. Small villages grew up and people grew maize (corn), beans, and pumpkins. Some of the earliest civilizations were also in this area: the Olmec culture with its center at La Venta, the Teotihuacan culture, and the beginnings of the Maya culture which lasted until about A.D. 1000.

► This little pottery figure of a crying baby is the work of the Olmec Amerindians who settled in communities on the coast of the Gulf of Mexico. Their center was at La Venta. They invented a type of hieroglyphic writing and a numerical system.

▼ Huge stone heads, some of them 9 feet tall and weighing 15 tons, were carved by the Olmecs. They are thought to represent gods. The Olmec sculptors also carved small figures out of jade and similar hard stone.

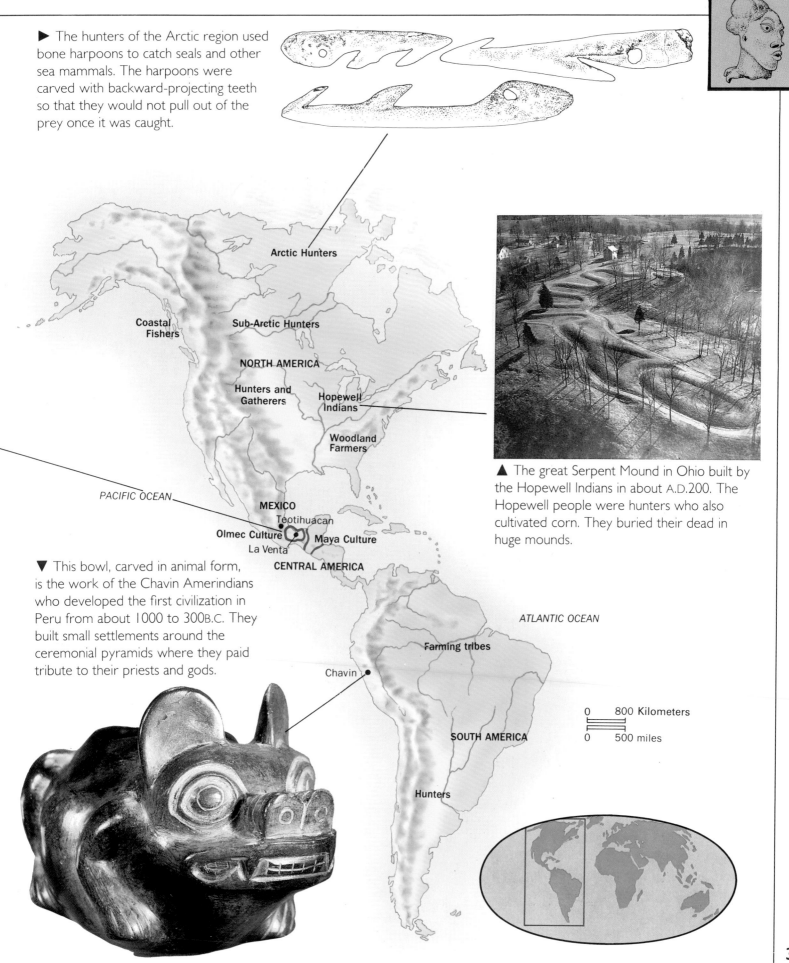

► The hunters of the Arctic region used bone harpoons to catch seals and other sea mammals. The harpoons were carved with backward-projecting teeth so that they would not pull out of the prey once it was caught.

Arctic Hunters

Coastal Fishers

Sub-Arctic Hunters

NORTH AMERICA

Hunters and Gatherers

Hopewell Indians

Woodland Farmers

PACIFIC OCEAN

MEXICO
Teotihuacan
Olmec Culture
La Venta
Maya Culture

CENTRAL AMERICA

▲ The great Serpent Mound in Ohio built by the Hopewell Indians in about A.D.200. The Hopewell people were hunters who also cultivated corn. They buried their dead in huge mounds.

▼ This bowl, carved in animal form, is the work of the Chavin Amerindians who developed the first civilization in Peru from about 1000 to 300B.C. They built small settlements around the ceremonial pyramids where they paid tribute to their priests and gods.

ATLANTIC OCEAN

Farming tribes

Chavin

0   800 Kilometers
0   500 miles

SOUTH AMERICA

Hunters

African Empires

Up until the end of the last ice age the area which we now call the Sahara was not desert but wet grassland. In this fertile region the early African peoples cultivated wheat and barley and herded cattle. But after about 2500B.C. the climate slowly became warmer and the Sahara began to dry out. Some of the farmers moved gradually southward to the **tropical** regions of the interior. Here, after about 2000B.C., sorghum, millet, and yams were cultivated: elsewhere, in places where the jungle was too thick for crop-growing, local economies were sometimes based on fishing.

The earliest African civilization south of the great Egyptian Empire (*see pages 16–18*) was the kingdom of Kush, which flourished on the banks of the Nile from about 500B.C. to A.D.350. Its capital, Meroë, was an important center for iron-working from about 500B.C., and this skill quickly spread south. People could now make iron tools and weapons, cultivation was easier and crop yields improved.

The Bantu peoples

South of the rain forests of the Congo Basin the earliest inhabitants were hunters; the San and the Khoi-khoi peoples. But gradually a new group of people migrated from their homeland in the north and west and developed their own cultures. They had one linking feature; their languages all came from **Bantu**.

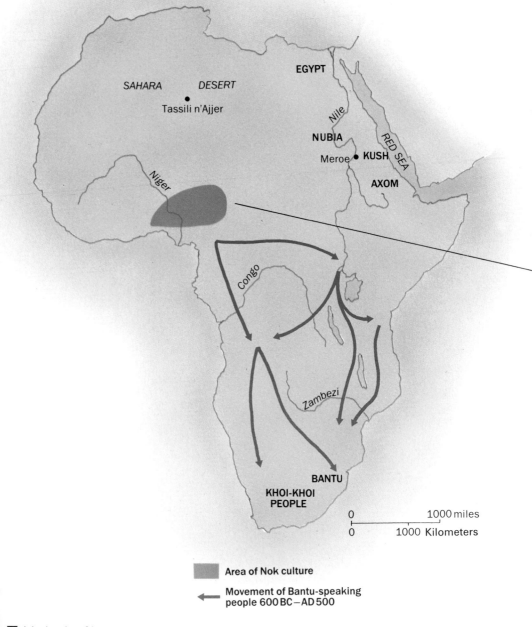

Area of Nok culture

Movement of Bantu-speaking people 600 BC – AD 500

▼ Methods of iron smelting were developed in Africa after about 500B.C. In this picture the furnace is built of compacted earth and bellows are used to reach the high temperatures necessary to turn the iron ore into metal. The metal produced was used to make strong tools and weapons.

40,000B.C.–A.D.456

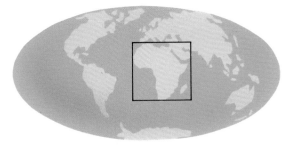

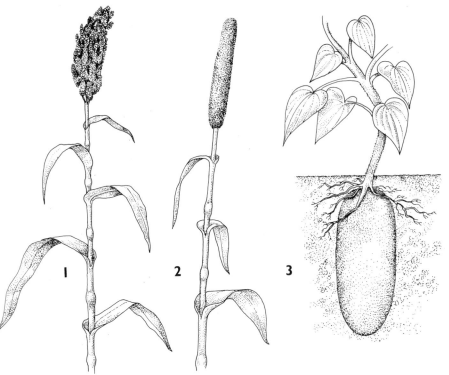

▼ One of the fine terracotta heads found near the village of Nok, in northern Nigeria. This type of sculpture flourished in the area from about 400 B.C. to A.D. 200.

▲ Three important crops which were cultivated by early farmers south of the Sahara.

1. Sorghum, an important early crop.
2. Millet, faster-growing than sorghum and able to withstand a drier climate.
3. Yam, a nutritious tuber.

▼ Rock paintings and relief carvings are found all over Africa. This lively cattle-herding scene comes from the Tassili-n-Ajjer Mountains in the Sahara. The first **pastoralists** in the Sahara region protected goats and sheep; later many different breeds of cattle were kept.

Australia and Oceania

The first people migrated to Australia between 70,000 and 50,000 years ago. At that time the sea levels were lower than they are today, so that Australia, New Guinea, and Tasmania were all joined by huge land bridges, forming a land mass called "Greater Australia." The first Australians, ancestors of the Aborigines, had to sail across the sea from southeast Asia to reach the nearest point of Greater Australia.

Around 6,000 years ago the sea rose to its present level, and the Aboriginal people began to move into the interior and exploit the natural resources found there. The Aborigines were fishers, hunters, and gatherers: they never developed a system of agriculture or cattle-rearing. They developed their own culture until the arrival of the Europeans in the A.D.1700s.

The smaller Pacific Islands which make up Oceania, spread out over the vast Pacific Ocean, were colonized much later. The first people sailed from the Moluccas region of Indonesia in about 2000B.C. These people were able to build large canoes that could survive long voyages, and transport not only them but their supplies, animals, and some of the plants they grew. They sailed first to the islands of Melanesia, then in about 1300B.C. they reached Fiji, Samoa, and Tonga. The farthest islands of Oceania, and New Zealand, were not settled until at least A.D.800.

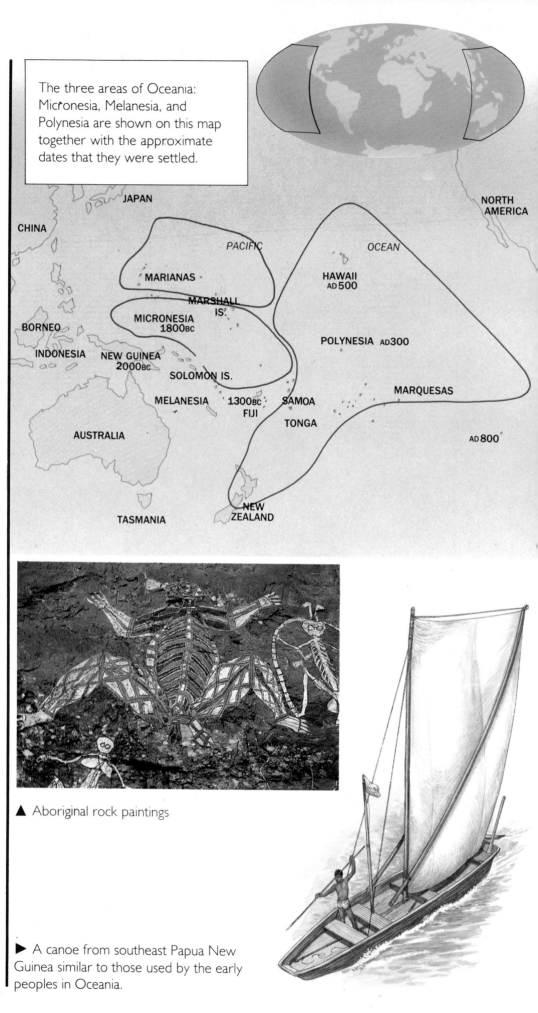

The three areas of Oceania: Micronesia, Melanesia, and Polynesia are shown on this map together with the approximate dates that they were settled.

▲ Aboriginal rock paintings

▶ A canoe from southeast Papua New Guinea similar to those used by the early peoples in Oceania.

40,000 B.C.–A.D.456

Glossary

Words in this book in **bold** are explained in the glossary below.

Agriculture The science of raising animals and growing crops.

Amphitheater An oval or circular open-air theater with seats around a central space.

Anthropology The scientific study of human beings.

Aqueduct A bridge built to carry water.

Archaeology The study of ancient buildings, tools, and other remains.

Aristocrat A noble man or woman.

Aryan The name given to the Indo-European invaders of India.

Bantu (means "people") A group of people from central and southern Africa who speak one of the Bantu languages.

Bronze An alloy (mixture) of copper and tin.

Citadel An elevated fortress protecting a city.

Citizen A person who lives in a town or city.

City state A city that is also an independent country.

Civilization A developed way of life including living in cities or towns.

Civil War A war between different groups in the same country.

Colony A settlement by people outside their own country, but ruled from their home country.

Consul One of the two Ancient Roman officials elected each year.

Culture The way of life of a particular group of people.

Democracy A country in which the government is chosen by the people.

Dynasty A line of rulers from the same family.

Empire A group of countries under one ruler.

Fossils Remains of ancient plants or animals, preserved as stone.

Glacials Periods when large areas of Earth were covered by ice: ice ages.

Hieroglyphs Writing using picture symbols.

Hominid A member of the family *Hominidae*, which includes modern humans and their ancestors.

Interglacials The warmer periods between glacials.

Irrigation Watering dry land to help crops grow.

Kiln A furnace used for firing pottery.

Kingdom A country ruled by a king or queen.

Land bridge A strip of land connecting two larger areas.

Mesoamerica A term for Mexico and Central America.

Neanderthals A group of early people who lived in Europe from about 100,000B.C. to 35,000B.C.

Nomads People who wander from place to place in search of food or grazing for their animals.

Oracle The means of consulting the gods about the future, or asking for advice.

Pastoralists People who herd and graze flocks of animals.

Pharaoh (means "great house") The title of the king of Egypt.

Primates A group of animals that includes humans and monkeys.

Republic A country with an elected government but no royal family.

Satrapies Administrative areas in ancient Persia.

Seals Cylinders engraved with a device which leaves an impression on soft wax.

Semitic languages The group of languages which includes modern Arabic, Aramaic, and Hebrew.

Senate A group of aristocrats in Rome who advised the consuls, or later the emperor.

Smelting The process of extracting metal by heating it to a high temperature.

Terracotta Unglazed, usually brownish-red pottery.

Trade The process of exchanging goods.

Tropics The areas of land around the Equator.

Vizier In Ancient Egypt the title of a chief minister or the governor of a province.

Ziggurat A type of pyramid built in ancient Babylonia.

 Europe	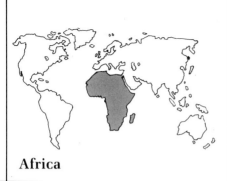 Near East	Africa
B.C. *c.***40,000** Last ice age *c.***33,000** Neanderthals die out *c.***20,000** Cave art flourishes in France and Spain *c.***2000** Minoans build Knossos in Crete *c.***1600** Beginning of Mycenean civilization in Greece *c.***1450** Destruction of Minoan civilization *c.***1100** Phoenician supremacy in the Mediterranean **900–750** Rise of city-states in Greece **776** First Olympic Games **753** Founding of Rome (traditional date) **481** Greeks defeat Persian invasion *c.***400** Athens rises to power in Greece **431–404** War between Athens and Sparta *c.***300** Rome rises to power in Italy **264–146** Punic wars between Rome and Carthage **27** Octavian becomes first Roman Emperor **A.D.** **330** City of Constantinople (Istanbul) founded **370** Huns from Asia invade Europe **395** Roman Empire divided in two	**B.C.** *c.***8000** First farming in Mesopotamia *c.***7000** Walls of Jericho built *c.***3500** Beginnings of Sumerian civilization *c.***3200** First writing in Sumeria **2360** Akkadian Empire founded by Sargon **1792–1750** Rule of Hammurabi, King of Babylon *c.***1500** Iron first smelted by the Hittites *c.***1200** Beginnings of Jewish religion *c.***1200** Israelites colonize Palestine *c.***721–705** Assyrian Empire at height of its power **586** Babylonian captivity of Jews *c.***500** Persian Empire at its height **334** Alexander the Great begins conquest of Persia **A.D.** *c.***30** Crucifixion of Jesus Christ **70** Romans destroy Jerusalem; *diaspora* (dispersal) of Jews begins **132** Jewish rebellion against Rome **226(–651)** Sassanians rule Persian Empire **330** Capital of Roman Empire transferred to Constantinople (Istanbul)	**B.C.** *c.***40,000** Earliest specimens of modern humans (*Homo sapiens*) found in Africa *c.***5000** Farming introduced into northern Africa *c.***3200** First Dynasty in Egypt *c.***2800** Pyramids of Giza begun *c.***2685** Beginning of "Old Kingdom" in Egypt *c.***2500** Sahara begins to dry out *c.***1570** Beginning of "New Kingdom" in Egypt *c.***900** Kingdom of Kush becomes independent of Egypt *c.***900** Nok culture of Nigeria begins **814** Phoenicians found colony at Carthage *c.***600** Iron smelting developed in northern Africa *c.***600** Bantu people move into southern Africa *c.***550** Arabs from Yemen colonize Ethiopia **332** Alexander the Great conquers Egypt **A.D.** **30** Egypt becomes a Roman province **350** Kingdom of Axum (Ethiopia) conquers Kush **350** Christianity reaches Ethiopia **429(–535)** Vandal Kingdom in northern Africa

Asia & the Far East	**The Americas**	**Australasia**

B.C. ***c.*6000** Rice cultivated in Thailand ***c.*2500–1500** Indus valley civilization ***c.*1500** Shang Dynasty in China **1028** Chou Dynasty in China ***c.*650** Introduction of iron working **563** Birth of the Buddha **551** Birth of Confucius	**B.C.** ***c.*40,000** First people migrate to America ***c.*15,000** Cave art practiced in Brazil ***c.*9000–7000** Flint arrowheads ("Folsom points") made in southern U.S.A. ***c.*4500** Farming develops in central America **3372** First date in Mayan calendar ***c.*1500** Stone temples built in Mesoamerica ***c.*1000** Chavín people of Peru making pottery ***c.*700** Stone city of Chavín de Huántar built ***c.*500** Gallinazo and Salinar cultures flourish in Peru	**B.C.** ***c.*50,000** First Aborigines arrive in Greater Australia ***c.*2000** First settlers arrive in New Guinea ***c.*1300** First settlers arrive in Fiji, Tonga, and Samoa
320–184 Mauryan Dynasty rules northern India **273–232** Asoka introduces Buddhism into southern India **221** Ch'in Dynasty in China **214** Great Wall of China completed **202** Han Dynasty in China		
A.D. **50**B.C.–A.D.**50** Buddhism introduced into China **220(–587)** Civil war in China (Six Dynasties period) **320(–500)** Gupta Dynasty rules northern India **360–390** Japanese conquer Korea	**A.D.** ***c.*100** Olmec civilization flourishes in Mesoamerica ***c.*200** Hopewell Indians build burial mounds in Ohio ***c.*300** Risa of Mayan civilization of Mesoamerica ***c.*500** Inuit begin hunting seals and whales	**A.D.** ***c.*300** First settlers arrive in Polynesia

Index

Page numbers in *italics* refer to illustrations

Acknowledgments

The publishers wish to thank the following for supplying photographs for this book:

Page 8 The Hutchison Library (top), Michael Holford (bottom); 10 Courtesy, French Government Tourist Office; 11 Ancient Art & Architecture Collection; 12 Sonia Halliday Photographs (top), Straatliche Museum, Berlin (bottom); 13 Sonia Halliday Photographs; 15 ZEFA (top), Ancient Art & Architecture Collection (bottom); 17 Spectrum Colour Library (top left), Michael Holford (top right), Fitzwilliam, Cambridge (bottom); 20 British Museum; 21 Sonia Halliday Photographs (top), The Hutchison Library (bottom); 23 The Hutchison Library; 24 Spectrum Colour Library; 25 Michael Holford; 27 ZEFA (top), Ancient Art & Architecture Collection (bottom); 28 Sonia Halliday Photographs; 30 Museum of Athens (top), Spectrum Colour Library (bottom); 31 Ekdotike Athenon (left), Michael Holford (right); 32 Michael Holford (top), Ancient Art & Architecture Collection (bottom); 33 The Hutchison Library (left), Michael Holford (right); 34 Sonia Halliday Photographs (top), Ancient Art & Architecture Collection (middle & bottom); 35 Sonia Halliday Photographs; 36 Werner Forman Archive (top), The Hutchison Library (bottom), 37 Museum of the American Indian, Heye Foundation (top), Werner Forman Archive (bottom); 39 The Hutchison Library; 40 The Hutchison Library.

Front Cover The Hutchison Library.
Back Cover The Hutchison Library. Michael Holford

Endpapers Austrian National Library, Vienna.

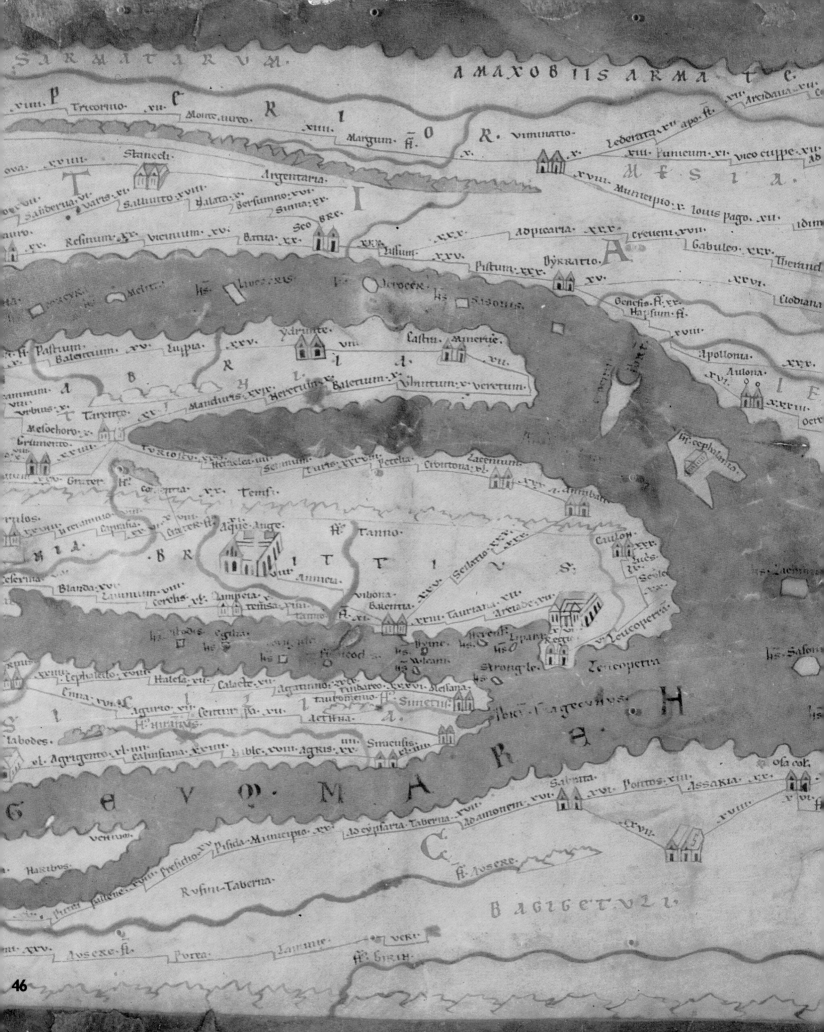